FAMILY- CAREER
CHOICES
A WOMAN'S PERSPECTIVE

This book is dedicated to my family, both immediate and extended.
Without them, this book and all my other endeavors
would not be possible.

FAMILY- CAREER
CHOICES
A WOMAN'S PERSPECTIVE

FAMILY- CAREER
CHOICES
A WOMAN'S PERSPECTIVE

Foreword:

As the title indicates, this book addresses the challenges working

women face today in trying to meet the demands of family, while still

maintaining a career. The book is intended for not only those women

who have children presently and are working outside or inside the

home, but also for those women who plan to have children at some

point and wish to attain an understanding of the issues and problems

they may face. Even those women who may not desire to have

children, but still place their husband and other family members as a

priority may benefit from this book. The last group that may find this

book useful are managers and supervisors of women who wish to gain

an understanding of the issues their female employees may face and how they can more effectively manage these women to maintain a better working environment for all.

The book is not intended to address all the issues working women face, as that would be too big an endeavor for any book to undertake. However, it will deal with some of the pertinent issues women face in trying to maintain their careers without their family life suffering. The book is based on some real life experiences and testimonies of women who have had to make some tough choices in order to be the type of wife and mother they desire to be. The author, herself, has experienced many of the issues addressed and has written this book in an effort to hopefully help other women deal with the concerns they may face. If nothing else, it should make each woman realize she is not alone in trying to "have it all." If at least one woman is helped by something in this book, then it will have served its purpose.

TABLE OF CONTENTS

TABLE OF CONTENTS

(CONTINUED)

"It is fun to have fun, but you have to know how."

CHAPTER I
INTRODUCTION

Just by reading the title, <u>Family - Career Choices, A Woman's Perspective</u>, you have already gained an understanding of the main message in this book. I believe that every woman can "Have it all", but what she has and when she has it requires making choices. From the time a child is born, that child's life is made up of choices: Do I keep crying or do I go to sleep? Do I continue to throw a temper tantrum or do I give up because no one is paying attention? It seems as adults, though, we sometimes forget that we too, have choices to make everyday; some of which may be life changing and some as simple as when and what to eat. However, when it comes to a woman taking charge of her future, we sometimes think we have to follow a certain path or to continue in a present job, when there really are alternatives. The question is, how do we take charge of our personal and family destinies?

Hopefully, reading this book will be a start for many women in trying to work through the choices they have to make if they are going to feel good about themselves and their family's structure and lifestyle. This book is going to lay out one method of trying to take hold of what each woman deserves: the right to direct her and her family's future. This statement does not mean to discount the role of fathers and husbands, as they are just as important to the overall success of the family and will play a large role in determining the support network of the mother or wife. However, in most families the mother in today's society still plays the dominant role as the caretaker and nurturer of the family, and this fact cannot be overlooked. For many career women, their toughest job begins after they walk out of the office.

In an effort to try to help each women assess herself, her present situation, and her support network, several questionnaires have been placed in the front of the chapters that correspond to these subjects.

These questionnaires should be answered prior to reading the chapter that follows. By reviewing the questions and choosing the best possible answer, a woman has begun her analysis phase. As she reads the chapter, she will see how these questions and her responses play a role in the choices she will make. Because of the nature of the questionnaires and the uniqueness of the responses for each situation, I have not provided any solutions to the questionnaires. Each woman will have to determine her own solutions based on what the responses she makes means to her situation. Because each woman has a unique set of circumstances surrounding her family and career, it would be difficult to impossible to try to interpret what each response means in every case. By answering "always" to certain questions and "never" to other questions, one woman may be guided toward a solution for attaining her balance that differs from the solution another woman finds who has answered the questions in a similar manner. One woman may be married with a supportive husband and another woman may not be married but have a very flexible job situation. If I attempted to provide solutions to these questionnaires, I fear I would be making the choices for a woman without knowing her unique set of circumstances. These questionnaires are a guide only to speed a woman through the analysis process, realizing that the women who will read this book do not have lots of spare time for quiet meditation. Seeing the questions and responses in black and white allows a women to continue her analysis, even when interruptions come into play.

Taking the fact that most women usually are the dominant caretaker and nurturer into consideration, it is not an easy role that every women has to play between balancing her family responsibilities along with her career responsibilities. We have to face the facts that as much as some women would like to stay home with their children, they just cannot, due to circumstances sometimes beyond their control. Single mothers with children to support and no supportive father have no choice other than to go to work. For other families with both a mother and father living at home, sometimes the father's salary may not be enough to make ends meet and extra income from the mother is needed. Some may argue that lifestyles can always be adjusted for these families, but that is not always the case. The situation also depends on what the parents agree on as their own personal minimum standard of life. For some families, just having a place to be safe and warm is enough, while for others a home or residence in a particular community is considered a necessity. If it is their children's safety that they are concerned about in wanting to live in that particular community and it takes both incomes just to maintain a modest household, then it is hard to argue that their lifestyle is extravagant and that the mother could stay at home. Other women just know their own capabilities and shortcomings and realize that their children are better cared for on a daily basis by an outside caretaker. The important criteria here -- which will be discussed further in the next chapter -- is that women should not judge each other, as each woman's personal choices should be respected whether or not they live up to the other one's standards. This does not imply that there are not minimum standards that must be met to ensure safety and stability of the family unit, but as long as the family and children are cared for and loved in a healthy environment, personal choices should be respected. If we women cannot do that amongst ourselves, then how can we expect others to understand and support the choices we make?

Before we move on to the heart of the book, I would like to make one further comment about women respecting each other's decisions. It seems as if the female community is divided into those women who stay at home and those women who work. This division is nonsense, since all wives and mothers have the same basic hardships and joys in trying to make their family life successful. All women want their husband and children to be happy and satisfied whether they have work interests outside the home or not. Whether or not a woman chooses to, and is fortunate enough to stay home with her children full-time, she still faces the same issues as the woman who works. Let's face it: in today's society, it is very hard for some women to be able to stay home and make ends meet. In many instances, staying home is a temporary choice. Because of factors beyond some women's control, the choices available to some women may not be as easily definable, and we need to allow each woman to define the choices for herself. All women need to unite and put away any envy, if we as a society are going to make family and career work together. It is human nature for us to always want the things we do not possess, which is why women who work are envious of women who stay home and visa versa. But the point of this book is that, however an individual woman can make family and career work best is the right choice for her.

QUESTIONNAIRE FOR CHAPTER II

ANALYZE YOURSELF

Questions for all women:

Never Sometimes Frequently Always   1. Do you feel a mother that works outside the home can have a positive effect on the development of children?

Never Sometimes Frequently Always   2. Are you opposed to having your children cared for in a daycare environment?

Never Sometimes Frequently Always   3. Do you question decisions you make just because someone expresses an opinion contrary to your own?

Never Sometimes Frequently Always   4. Do you enjoy the stimulation you receive from working outside the home?

Never Sometimes Frequently Always   5. In an ideal world, would you choose to stay at home?

Never Sometimes Frequently Always   6. Would you rather be working outside the home on a part-time basis.

Never Sometimes Frequently Always   7. Do you feel like it is necessary for children to be home with one of their parents after the school day is over?

Never Sometimes Frequently Always   8. Are their other children in your neighborhood that your children can play with?

Never Sometimes Frequently Always   9. Do you feel you would enjoy the interaction from others in a working environment.

Never Sometimes Frequently Always   10. Do you get real nervous when your child cries or complains a lot?

Never Sometimes Frequently Always   11. Do you have a low tolerance level for the confusion sometimes associated with the activities of children?

Never Sometimes Frequently Always   12. Do you find that you listen to your intuition, especially as it relates to the needs of your family?

Never Sometimes Frequently Always   13. When you review the last ten years, can you see some of the changes in your perspective toward career and family?

Never Sometimes Frequently Always   14. Do you feel you are the major nurturer in your family?

Never Sometimes Frequently Always   15. Do you feel your children are at an age where they need you or are they more self-sufficient?

Questions for women who work outside the home:

Never Sometimes Frequently Always 16. Do you require the mental or physical stimulation that you receive by being asked to perform a job in a certain way?

Never Sometimes Frequently Always 17. Do you feel good when others feel like your efforts have contributed to the success of their project?

Never Sometimes Frequently Always 18. Do you view the work you do outside the home as a career you are proud of?

Never Sometimes Frequently Always 19. Do you work outside the home to fulfill a financial need only?

Never Sometimes Frequently Always 20. Do you feel like you are just at the start of your career?

Never Sometimes Frequently Always 21. Were you eager to return to work after the birth of your children?

Never Sometimes Frequently Always 22. Have your feelings toward your job changed since you had children?

Never Sometimes Frequently Always 23. Are you frustrated by the hours you are required to spend in your work environment?

Never Sometimes Frequently Always 24. Do you feel you have satisfied your career goals and want to devote more time to family matters?

Never Sometimes Frequently Always 25. If possible, would you want to take some time off from work right now?

Questions for women who are married only:

Never Sometimes Frequently Always 26. Does your husband prefer for you to work outside the home?

Never Sometimes Frequently Always 27. Do you and your spouse require both incomes to meet your financial needs?

Never Sometimes Frequently Always 28. Are you aware of your husband's priorities?

Never Sometimes Frequently Always 29. Is your husband very conscientious about finances concerning your retirement and future needs?

Never Sometimes Frequently Always 30. Is the income earned from your job used to pay monthly bills, instead of simply spending money?

Never Sometimes Frequently Always 31. Do you and your spouse frequently argue about finances?

Never Sometimes Frequently Always 32. Does your spouse place a great deal of emphasis on the money you make?

CHAPTER II
ANALYZE YOURSELF

Before any woman can effectively deal with the choices she must make regarding her family and career, she must have done a thorough analysis of herself. This analysis involves determining how she truly feels about her family and career preferences. She must also determine the real reasons why she works and what her true priorities are. The feelings most women have toward their careers will change over time, and they need to be aware of and accept this fact. Before a woman can move to the next stage in positioning her career to meet her family situation, she must be aware of and feel good about her own feelings as they relate to the choices she will make.

The question is, how do you begin to analyze yourself? The process is really quite easy and is actually being performed informally by most women on a regular basis. As women are constantly faced with pressures from society in trying to establish an identity, most women know deep in their hearts what their true feelings are. The media constantly produces articles and programs about the positive and negative effects of working mothers on the development of children. In one program, the experts may say children will grow up emotionally unstable because they were put in a daycare situation early in life; and then in the next program or article, another expert may announce that mothers working outside the home instill confidence and a strong sense of individualism. Because women are getting mixed signals and hearing debates over this issue of outside careers on a daily basis, most women have formed an opinion whether they realize it or not. One key step in making the choices to get the desired family/career mix involves identifying that opinion.

In trying to identify her true feelings toward her family and career, a woman must first put aside all the opinions expressed to her by others. Even though I mentioned above the pressures from the media, far greater pressures are exerted from family and friends every day. Relatives and friends are always ready to express their views on what worked for them and how you should handle any situation. These views are not always negative and should not be viewed that way. These people care about you and truly want the best for you and your family just as you do. The problem is that either you may be unsure of your own feelings and course of action, or their opinions could be outdated and not fit your situation at all. When faced with all these opinions and recommendations the best course of action to take is to accept them graciously, and then do with them as you please. If they make sense to you and you see some real use, then store these views in your mind for later applicability. If they make no sense to you and have no real use or meaning for your life, then create a garbage can in your mind and discard them there. The important thing here is to decide for yourself how you feel and what works for you.

Now that we have addressed the issue of putting aside messages sent to you from the media, family and friends, you are ready to begin to look inside yourself to determine how you feel about your family and career goals. You need to ask yourself in an ideal situation, "What do I really want for myself and my family." Now, we all know everyone's first answer is win the lottery and be able to afford to do anything we want to do! Even though this may be a nice dream to have, we women have to look at this question realistically. I know that personally speaking, my response would be that I love to work, but that I would like to be able to work only when I feel like it or it fits my family situation. Since this idea is also somewhat a dream, I have to narrow that desire down to a more realistic level. Maybe by being my own boss, I can dictate my own hours; however, if I am earning money for providing some goods or services, than I have to face the fact that I must be willing to meet my customers' needs. If I do not meet their needs, they are not going to be willing to pay me and will not provide me any future business. So, even though I may like to work only when

I want to, I have to arrive at a compromise that will allow me to try to schedule my hours so that I can, for the most part, do the things that I would like to do and try to achieve a situation which allows flexibility.

For me attaining the working conditions I needed meant leaving a full-time job, where I felt the mentality was such that I would never be able to gain the hours and flexibility needed, and going to a part-time job with some other possible contract work. The bottom line for me is that I wanted to be able to pick my son up from school and have the afternoons to spend with him and my two other boys. Since my oldest son was in elementary school, my second son was just starting kindergarten, and my youngest son seemed happy in his preschool class, I did not mind -- and actually enjoyed -- working most mornings, and would have been willing to work other hours as it fit my children's schedules. I also was trying to reserve at least one day a week to keep my youngest son home so that I could capture those last days before he would also have to attend school. But in our neighborhood, there are no other small children, so I felt they would be bored staying home with just me every day: I felt like the interaction with other children his age in preschool was necessary, helpful, and enjoyable for him.

The opinions expressed above are my feelings, only. How you feel and what you choose may be entirely different, and that is fine. If all women felt the same way, we would not have all the varying contributions provided from women that we have today. In terms of what you may want for yourself related to a career, you need to ask yourself if you really derive satisfaction from your job. **Do you enjoy interacting with others in a working environment? Do you feel good when others feel that your efforts have contributed to the success of their project? Do you require the mental or physical stimulation that you receive by being asked to perform a job in a certain way?** If you answer yes to at least one of the questions above that you have probably determined that you like to be in a working environment. So for you, some semblance of work not only satisfies a financial need, but also an emotional need. You view your job as a career that you are proud to be associated with. If you could not answer yes, you probably are working to fulfill a financial need only and would really prefer to be working in the home full-time or working in another career field. How you feel about the reasons you work is your own thought-out opinion.

How do you feel your family unit should be structured?
Here again, try to look within yourself, blocking out messages and opinions of others. First, we must all admit that we are not all "June Cleavers." Neither are all our husbands "Ward Cleavers," nor do our children always nicely do as we ask and remember to wash their hands before dinner. For some women the "Cleaver family" may be an ideal setup they want to strive for, but other women may want more of an independent life. During my mother's era of having children, most women stayed at home. She was never really faced with the issue of

balancing career and family. She was a good wife and mother, which was just what she wanted to do. Even as times change, my mother has kept the concept of family close to my heart, even though she realizes that career plays a role in my life also. This issue is where women, for the most part, become divided, and sometimes hostile feelings develop toward other women. These feelings need to be put aside in an effort for tolerance, along with the messages from others that you have decided have no applicability for you. For many women, the first time they are faced with this issue is while they are on maternity leave. As many women will say regarding their newborn child, something happens inside them once that baby is born, and their life never is the same again. Even women who had every intention of returning to employment outside the home and were very career oriented find themselves exploring the issue of whether they want to or should remain at home with their child.

When I returned from work after having my first child, I can remember people telling me that they thought I had changed, and that my emphasis had definitely shifted. For me, I know it was a change for the better, as my career took a backseat to my family. For some of you women, this same change occurred or will occur. Most women I have talked to noticed a real change or emphasis in their feelings toward family life after the birth of their first child. Along with these changes in emotions, most women are amazed at the amount of time a newborn baby requires in order to meet his/her daily needs. The time constraints alone can make it seem impossible to accomplish the tasks they were able to complete, assuming they would like to get some sleep. Some women may become so overwhelmed with the constant demands of a newborn that they are eager to get back to work after their child is born and launch full throttle into their career again. They have missed the challenges and companionship of the workplace. With these differing points of view in mind, we should put aside any tendency to determine which mother is the better or more devoted parent. This personal decision by each women should be respected, unless you have walked in that other woman's shoes for a day.

In my opinion, if a woman knows that she does not have the patience for her child or can barely stand to hear the crying until her husband can come home and take over, then the child is probably better off being taken care of by someone who has the love and patience a newborn child requires. The same thing can be said about young or teenage children, as some mothers find different ages more tolerable and enjoyable. I believe some people are gifted caregivers and for others it is a struggle. For a woman to realize her shortcomings and do what is best for her child shows just as much love as the woman who chooses to stay home full-time with her child. Each person needs to look within herself and determine her tolerance level for her children and herself. I will be the first to admit that even though I love my children, I feel it is good for them and me both to spend a little time with others who can provide us with a different kind of stimulation.

That does not mean I do not miss them when they are away from me, or that I do not think or talk about them all the time. I enjoy the mental stimulation I receive from performing my profession, just as I feel that they enjoy the mental stimulation they receive from learning letters, numbers, music, and art with their fellow preschool students. Each woman has to identify who she really is and wants to be regarding her family, and to become comfortable with that identity.

During this self-analysis phase, which I feel is probably the most important process a woman goes through when she is trying to determine the choices she must make regarding her family and career, each individual has to review her priorities and -- if she is married -- her husband's priorities. Each family has its own set of priorities, most of the time based upon events of the past and feelings that have built up over time during each of the parent's own childhood and development.

When a husband is involved, the wife cannot simply examine her own priorities without reconciling or acknowledging the differences in priorities experienced between her and her husband. Raising the children and developing the kind of home life a woman desires is a cooperative effort between wife and husband, when she is married. Some husbands may be reluctant to announce their priorities, while others may be very vocal. In either case, a woman should not be fooled into thinking her husband does not have his own desired plan for life, and his own set of priorities for how his family life should be structured. I have a very supportive husband, who has given me freedom to establish some goals for the structure of our family life.

However, I realize there are constraints on those goals if I want my marriage to be successful and my home life to be happy. One of those constraints is that my husband is very conscientious when it comes to debt management. Even though this feeling is partly connected with his career in banking, I know it also comes from the values presented to him by his parents, who also were very frugal. Because of this feeling, and the fact that he too, wants to spend time with his children, I have to be realistic in assuming that I will have to share in the burden of earning enough income to meet our expense structure.

How we organize that expense structure is beyond the scope of this book, other than mentioning that we have to come to a consensus about how our income will be allocated among both sets of priorities. In other words, the income that will be needed to maintain the lifestyle that both the husband and wife desire and how it will be spent are determinations that need to be made through the process of defining a family budget. In this book, I am not attempting to set out a financial plan or discuss the family budgeting process. However this planning for financial needs is an important consideration that cannot be ignored when a woman is considering her and her husband's priorities. The bottom line is that in analyzing oneself, a woman cannot forget or ignore her husband's priorities and situation; because if she is married, his priorities become her priorities too.

The last key concept in a woman's self analysis involves recognizing for herself at what stage in her life she is presently at. This statement means that we all know that, just as our family life is constantly evolving and changing; we, as women, are changing too. The desires we feel today will not necessarily be the same desires we will feel tomorrow. I can remember in an "Organizational Behavior and Development" course I took when I was pursuing my masters degree, the textbook, Organizational Behavior and Management by Henry L. Tosi and W. Clay Hamner, discussed how managers need to be responsive to their employees by recognizing the stages of life that their individual employees are going through. Only through this consideration of life stages could they determine the best method of management, understanding how perceptions of careers and self change during adulthood. The textbook discussed the life structure as going through a sequence of alternating stable periods and transitional periods, with stable periods lasting 6 - 8 years and transitional periods lasting 4 - 5 years. During stable periods, a person would make crucial choices, build a life structure surrounding them, and seek to attain goals and values within this structure. During a transitional period, a person would seek to terminate the existing structure and work toward an initiation of a new structure. Tosi and Hamner theorized in this textbook that the reason we go through these developmental transitions in adulthood is that no life structure can permit the living out of all aspects of a person's life.

The instructor in the organizational behavior course stated that some preliminary research indicated that for women the age 26 was similar to a man in his late 30s. The textbook used in this course called the stage beginning at age 36 - 37 for a man the "BOOM" period, which stood for "Becoming One's Own Man." During this time a man wants to be more independent and more true to his wishes, even if they contradict his external demands. At the same time, he wants

affirmation, respect, and reward from the world that surrounds him.

This "BOOM" period takes a man from the culmination of early

adulthood in his late thirties into his mid-life transition. In his mid-life

transition a man questions his life structure, he reviews his successes

and failures making decisions regarding how he wants the rest of his

life to go.

In addition, the textbook described how men in their early

twenties are very career-oriented, striving to climb the corporate

ladder. In the late forties and early fifties a man typically is winding

down and considering his retirement years. Even though the textbook

was structured toward the male population, it still brought home the

concept that people at different ages want and need different things.

From my own personal experience, I know that in my early 20s,

I was very career oriented. At the age of 27 I had my first child and my emphasis changed. My number one priority was no longer trying to climb the corporate ladder as quickly as possible, but maintaining a career that would allow me to devote the time and care needed for my growing family. I can remember as I made this change in emphasis that my selection of opportunities was guided more towards those that would allow me to stay in town and on a consistent schedule. Before this time, I would have searched out the biggest challenge, even if it involved six weeks out-of-town at a time -- which one project I previously worked on required such. I definitely put more of an emphasis on the location and schedule that surrounded a job.

From that point on I went through a period of five years where it seemed I was either pregnant or nursing, as I gave birth to my other two sons. At the beginning of this time, I made a change within the consolidated company to a position that provided me with a shorter work day. Even though I enjoyed the job and was able to grow in my career, the change to the position was motivated in part by the chance for reduced working hours. I can remember comments made to me and about me that I was on the "mommy track". Even if these comments were sometimes made in jest, it still brought home the concept that management felt my devotion to my career was not as strong as they desired. At one point, I was even offered a position paying a great deal more if I would be willing to work at least a forty-hour week. When I turned the position down, management was disappointed and did not understand how I could turn down such an opportunity. However, the opportunity for me to be with my children provided greater satisfaction than any job could provide.

Now that I am in my mid 30s, my emphasis has continued to shift away from an importance on career and more towards the activities of my children. Through the last few years I have realized that my children will only be young once, and that I can "climb the corporate ladder" at any time. Even though I enjoy working, I know that at the present time, my children need me far more than any company could ever need me. Someone else could fill my shoes at the office, but no one else could fill my shoes as the mother to my children. A very successful woman in the public accounting profession recently told me that she could get all the clients she wanted to, but that she was passing her new clients on to other accountants because she had all the work she wanted right now. Even though she had never intended to have children, she was blessed with one and then another, and she just did not want to be away from them too much. For her, the age factor was not as much as a determinant as her family status. I think with most women that would be the case; since, women still seem to be the major nurturer in most families. So in trying to analyze oneself, one must realize such analysis will be a constant process and not a one time deal. Keep in mind that as your needs change, so will your choices regarding family and career. What you need to decide now is at what point you are at the present time. **Do you feel your children are at an age where they need you more or are they more self sufficient? Do you want to take more time off now while they are young or**

wait until they reach those teenage years? These are decisions that should be based on analyzing how you feel right now.

In summarizing , I want to reiterate that this chapter is probably the single most important part of this book, because any choices have to be based on a firm understanding and appreciation of oneself. One has to be proud of and at the same time realize her weaknesses, if she is to make the best choices for herself and her family. A woman's intuition will be her best guide to understanding herself. If a woman will listen to her intuition, she will correctly assess the situation in most cases. Some people have described intuition as divine guidance that protects us from uncomfortable or untrue situations. However you choose to describe your intuition, do not ignore it or you will probably find yourself at odds with the choices you will make later on. Listen to your heart and know first what you really want for yourself and your family. Then, understand what role career plays in your personal profile and where your priorities lie. Do not forget that a husband or significant other plays a role in establishing your priority structure.

Lastly, realize that you and your needs and wants are changing and

that you must consider those changes as you start to make the choices

that will move your family and career in the desired direction.

QUESTIONNAIRE FOR CHAPTER III

ANALYZE YOUR PRESENT SITUATION

Questions for all women:

Never Sometimes Frequently Always   1.   Do you feel like you are trapped by your present situation?

Never Sometimes Frequently Always   2.   Do you feel like your present life is running you instead of you running your life?

Never Sometimes Frequently Always   3.   Whether you are working inside or outside the house are you satisfied with your present situation?

Never Sometimes Frequently Always   4.   Do you feel the needs of your children are greater now and over the next few years?

Never Sometimes Frequently Always   5.   Do you need to be available in the afternoons for your children to be involved in outside activities?

Never Sometimes Frequently Always   6.   Do you feel you are giving your children enough of your time and attention?

Never Sometimes Frequently Always   7.   Do you feel you are aware of and able to meet most of your family's needs and requirements?

Never Sometimes Frequently Always   8.   Are you receiving signals from your children that their emotional needs may or may not be met?

Never Sometimes Frequently Always   9.   Do you feel you have ample time to be involved in your children's school and extracurricular activities?

Never Sometimes Frequently Always   10.   Are you involved in a lot of community or social activities that takes you away from your family?

Never Sometimes Frequently Always   11.   If you would like to pursue a career outside the home, will you need extra education or training to find the type of career you think will be family-friendly?

Never Sometimes Frequently Always   12.   If you need extra education, will you be able to obtain it?

Questions for women who work outside the home:

Never Sometimes Frequently Always   13.   Do you feel like the nature of your job is conducive to a working mother?

Never Sometimes Frequently Always   14. Do you spend a lot of your time commuting to and from work?

Never Sometimes Frequently Always   15. Are you satisfied with the physical location of your present work environment?

Never Sometimes Frequently Always   16. Is your work outside the home in close proximity to your home and your children's school?

Never Sometimes Frequently Always   17. Would you describe your management as having a more conventional, business-centered philosophy?

Never Sometimes Frequently Always   18. Do you feel that your management supports the family substructure?

Never Sometimes Frequently Always   19. Does your company support many family-centered activities?

Never Sometimes Frequently Always   20. Overall do you feel the management of the company supports women in their efforts to balance career and family?

Never Sometimes Frequently Always   21. Do you see any women with families in the upper management of your company?

Never Sometimes Frequently Always   22. Do you see any women in your office with flexible work arrangements?

Never Sometimes Frequently Always   23. If any women have flexible arrangements, did they have to ask for the benefits instead of being naturally entitled to them?

Never Sometimes Frequently Always   24. Do you know of any women who have requested flexible work arrangements and were turned down?

Never Sometimes Frequently Always   25. Do managers appear nervous or uncomfortable whenever flexible or reduced hours are discussed?

Never Sometimes Frequently Always   26. Does your company have any formal policies concerning flexible work arrangements?

Never Sometimes Frequently Always   27. Has your management allowed any women employees to leave, when it was known they were leaving because of inflexible work arrangements?

Never Sometimes Frequently Always   28. Do you hear talk among female employees of the company's inability to work with family issues?

Never Sometimes Frequently Always   29. Have any women that you know left the company prior to starting a family because they felt they would not be supported later?

Never Sometimes Frequently Always   30. If you have tried, do you feel you are put off every time you try to discuss flexible work arrangements?

Never Sometimes Frequently Always   31. Do you feel your management states they support family issues, but when it comes down to key decisions and actions, they send another message?

Never Sometimes Frequently Always   32. Do you feel your senior management is generally negative toward the issue of women having babies?

Never Sometimes Frequently Always   33. If you have children already, do you feel you are viewed as not as dedicated or loyal when you leave work either on-time or early to handle family problems?

Never Sometimes Frequently Always   34. Do you encounter travel in your job situation that causes problems in meeting the needs of your family?

Never Sometimes Frequently Always   35. When you have to travel and be away from home, do you notice negative effects on your children or their behavior?

Never Sometimes Frequently Always   36. Does your spouse's employment take him out-of-town, where travel in your job causes a major problem?

Never Sometimes Frequently Always   37. Do you frequently have to work long hours in your job that takes away time from your family?

Never Sometimes Frequently Always   38. Are you resentful of your management for the long hours you have to work?

Never Sometimes Frequently Always   39. Are you asked to stay late sometimes without advance notice?

Never Sometimes Frequently Always   40. Does your management make it known that they expect overtime on a regular basis?

Never Sometimes Frequently Always   41. Does your management work long hours on a regular basis?

Never Sometimes Frequently Always   42. Do you feel your management has unreasonable expectations in regards to the workload that can be accomplished in a normal work day?

Never Sometimes Frequently Always   43. If most of your senior management is male, do most of their wives work inside the home?

Never Sometimes Frequently Always   44. When working mothers have to be out-of-work because of sick children or other child-related needs, do you hear negative comments made by managers?

Never Sometimes Frequently Always   45. Does your job require you to put your physical safety at risk?

Never Sometimes Frequently Always   46. Does your employer offer educational opportunities for its employees at minimal or no cost?

Never Sometimes Frequently Always   47. Do you take advantage of educational opportunities offered by your employer?

CHAPTER III

ANALYZE YOUR PRESENT SITUATION

In this chapter, we will be exploring how to analyze your present situation to determine how your current job and family status fit into the balance you determined was necessary in the previous chapter. What amazes me most from my personal experience is how many women feel trapped by their present situation. Just recently, a friend of mine had her third child. When I asked if she was going to take off some time or work at home for a period of time like she did with her second child, she said she could not because the situation surrounding her job had changed. Even though her company was involved in several acquisitions that might make this work accommodation a little more difficult, one of the primary factors was a change in the management structure. Throughout this chapter we will attempt to identify the factors you have to consider when determining whether you will have to make a major change from your present situation, or whether merely modifying a few variables in it could make it manageable for you.

One of the first variables you have to identify in your present situation is whether you are working inside or outside the home and if the work situation is more of a release or a stressor for you. If you are working at home, but truly wish to be working outside the house, then this situation could be a stressful for you. Whether you are performing telecommuting-type work or are a stay-at-home mom, you may still feel a need for some outside interaction. If this need is too strong, than working at home can be a stressor for you. Likewise, if you are working outside the house, but truly wish to be working at home, then this could create stress in your life. Thus, the physical location -- where you reside for most of your day in performing your given tasks-- and type of work --telecommuting or stay-at-home mom -- are factors you must consider in analyzing your present situation.

Along these lines, consider the woman who lives outside a large metropolitan area, but has to drive into the city every day for work. Her children attend a school near their home, thus it takes her an hour to get to the school from her job. Despite these factors, she loves her job. However, because she wishes to be nearer to her children's school and school activities, she knows she must make a major change in her job situation. Her alternatives are to either work inside her home or find a job nearer to her house. Because she is a receptionist, she chooses a job near her house, even though it may not pay as much nor provide her the same level of satisfaction. The woman I knew who was faced with this situation had a hard time making the decision to leave her present employer, as she truly loved her job. However, the need to be close to her children overrode her need for her present position. Another woman I know solved this dilemma by becoming a court reporter, where she could do much of her work at home. One may not realize it, but the physical location of a job can be a major factor that needs to be assessed in analyzing your present situation.

If you are working for someone else, another important aspect of your present situation involves the management's philosophies and operating policies. Speaking from present experience, I have worked under both a supportive, family-centered management philosophy and under an older, conventional, business-centered management philosophy. In large part how I was able to balance family and career was affected by the management I operated under. Under the family-centered management philosophy, I was able to perform my job effectively, while at the same time meeting the needs of my family life. For me, life was wonderful at this time but the company went through a reorganization, and I was given a position at an affiliated company where I later encountered a less supportive management philosophy.

During part of the time spent with this affiliated employer, I truly enjoyed the work in my job. The problem was that the travel and other demands of the job took too much of my time away from my family. One example of an event that threw up a red flag for me that a problem was in the making, was the time I had gone over to Atlanta on a business day trip. The plane was scheduled to leave in time for me to be back in town to pick up my children from their preschool. However, because of the traffic at the airport, I sat on the runway for close to an hour. By the time we left, I was already too late to pick up my children. My husband did not know whether he needed to pick up the children, but luckily left work in time to get to the preschool before it closed. By the time I arrived in town, tensions were high all around. Needless to say the rest of the evening was stressed because of the events of the day and the uncertainty of everyone's responsibilities. Even the best planning could not eliminate all the problems that resulted. Because I had performed the self-evaluation discussed in the previous chapter, I knew I would have to make a major change in my job situation, which I subsequently did.

What many managers do not realize is that they lose many employees who could have made great contributions to their company when they do not allow for flexibility and family-centered work environments. In my previous situation, many women felt as if the department and company sent out a message that you could not have a family and successful career at the same time. Because of this feeling, many women had either left or were contemplating leaving prior to starting a family. I know of several women in particular that left because their family life was suffering. One woman in particular left because she was trying to start a family and had been unsuccessful. After leaving the stressful situation at her current work environment, she became pregnant in a matter of months. What a shame to lose that kind of experience and knowledge of the company!

If your management, through its actions, does not demonstrate a willingness to work with the female employee and to allow flexibility, a woman who needs this flexibility for her family/career balance has been given no choice but to leave. If you determine that you will need flexibility and shorter hours to make your family life work, evaluate whether your management will work with you, looking at their past actions and not just the words. Many managers can talk the talk, but if they do not walk the walk, the words are meaningless. Many managers have learned key words and phrases that they use to appease their female employees, but they are carefully phrased to be non-binding. You have to look past the words and at the actions. If there are no other female employees with families and who have flexible benefits, that probably demonstrates at the least the standard 8-to-5 mentality. In fact today because of the competitive environment of the workplace, most companies want more than a forty-hour work week out of their employees. Many employers are looking for a "company first" mentality from their employees.

However, you must realize that the problem with flexible work arrangements could also be the result of no one having asked or having felt bold enough to ask. But the fact that you are having to ask, or that women are afraid to ask may be an indicator, in itself, that the manager does not support flexible work arrangements. Even so, the old adage that it never hurts to ask, may be true in this case. If you decide to ask, be careful to look past the words your manager is saying, and look at his/her body language when you are asking, to tell if this could really be a successful arrangement. Experience is always your best indicator: look at what other women have done in the past and how they have been treated. If management has repeatedly allowed women to leave, and have not provided other flexible arrangements, you are probably not going to be too successful, either. At that point, you have to decide if you need to make a move. I can say from experience that there is nothing more frustrating than beating your head against a proverbial wall because your management keeps fighting you on all efforts to balance your family and career needs. If your management, through all indicators -- directly to you or others -- shows signs of resistance to flexible arrangements, do not waste your time and effort there. Move on to another situation and save your time and effort for your family and a work environment that will be more supportive, because there are other employers out there just waiting for your talents.

The good news for most women is that just because a woman puts her family first does not mean she will not encounter financial success. Contrary to this notion is a study conducted at the University of Pennsylvania Wharton School of Business in Philadelphia, which asked 2,140 men and 2,128 women if they considered marriage and family "very important", "somewhat important", or "not important" to their happiness. The study then tracked their earning power for 14 years after high school and found those who had answered "very important" wound earning about 7 percent more than those who had said "not important". The findings here contradict that a person who puts career first will have more financial success. One reason cited for the conclusions of the study are that the "not important" people had a higher divorce rate. In addition as most of us have observed, marital conflict and other personal problems can mess up a person's professional life.

Another factor to note when considering your present job situation involves the nature of the job in which you are currently working. I previously mentioned the job position I was given at the affiliated employer that involved travel. The job would have been great for a single person or a married person whose spouse either traveled or worked long hours, so that time away from the home was not an issue. Some jobs that are simply not suited to a person who has a firm commitment to home and her children. A woman I know told me recently she had just made a job change because she was having to leave her home on Monday and not return until Thursday. She said this situation was creating a discipline problem with her son, and it was just not working for her to be away from her home that much. Facing the fact that a job you enjoy may have to be put aside because of family commitments is a tough decision for any woman to make. The important thing is that it has to be the woman's decision after she has analyzed her priorities and knows that it is a sacrifice she must make. For someone in her family or her friends to tell her to quit her job would only cause hard feelings and not give her the power it will take to leave the job.

One woman I have known for quite a time just made a difficult choice because she found her work situation no longer tolerable. She has two children, one of them is grown and the other will be off at college in approximately two years. She is a dedicated employee who has been with her company for more than ten years. Because of the nature of her job, she is on-call almost any time of the day or night. Recently when her daughter asked her to go with her somewhere one evening, she told her she had to work. The daughter remarked to the effect that all her life all she had heard was the company's name and she did not know why her mother had children. Because the daughter is a teenager, the comment was probably made out of emotion and disappointment. However, the mother received the message loud and clear that she truly was not spending enough time with her daughter. Since her daughter would be gone in a few short years, she decided it was time to find a job situation that would allow her more stable hours and more time off. She was tired of calling herself "the woman without a life." She was tired of being a one-man team and went to work where she would be part of a team and maintain a normal schedule. She felt like the nature of the job at this particular company would not allow her the work schedule she needed.

One of the positions I have held in the past was an Acquisitions Coordinator. Due to the nature and activities of this job, I found it to be a very pleasant experience for me in many ways. The problem was that I knew for the job to be performed properly there would be times when I needed to be away from home, possibly a week at a time. Because I knew my family was my priority and I needed to be home, I had no choice but to leave the job. The important thing for most women to realize, if they have to make this type of sacrifice, is that if the opportunity was available once it will be available again. Few jobs can ever be classified as once in a lifetime experiences. As one woman told me, " I always said that, when the time was right, the job would be there -- and it always was!" **Can we say the same thing about missed opportunities with our children?**

In addition, there may be other jobs that do not involve travel, but may involve putting oneself at risk or simply spending long hours away from home at a time. A police woman or firefighter might put herself at risk, just as opening a restaurant may require long hours away from the home. The important criteria here is that, if the nature of this job conflicts with what you have determined to be your desired family/career balance, than you will have to take action to remedy the situation.

While evaluating your present situation, you also need to look at the type of career you have established for yourself. **Is the career conducive to the type of family structure you desire? What kind of education or training will be needed to change to another, more family-friendly career selection?** We all know that certain careers require more education than others, and that others will require both education and extensive training. If you feel your chosen career does not meet your needs, than you will need to consider the time and financial demands that may be required to change to another career path. Many courses can be taken at night, but schooling may require some temporary sacrifices from yourself and your family . Whether you are currently happy in your current career or are considering a change in career, you need to take advantage of all educational opportunities available to you. Many companies will finance their employees' tuition and/or books at local colleges for them to gain additional knowledge. Other courses or seminars may be available at either no cost or a very nominal cost. Still other employers, especially large companies, may provide training courses on-site and during working hours that will allow their employees to gain additional skills.

I am a firm believer that all people should obtain as much knowledge as possible in order to keep expanding their horizons and to provide themselves with more opportunities. You will only be limited by yourself and what you are willing to do, especially if opportunities are available at no cost and within your normal working hours. If your opportunities for increased education are limited or cannot be worked into your present lifestyle without great sacrifice, then you will need to either consider a change within your present career or a different career that will not demand additional training prior to employment. You may not always be able to select your first choice of careers at the present time, but maybe the alternative career choice can meet your needs in the interim with nothing more than some on-site training.

Continuing with the process of analyzing your present situation, you must also look at factors other than those related to your career that have been previously discussed. These issues would be those relating to your family needs. Everyone knows that when children are small, they require a lot of time and monitoring by their parents. However, as parents of teenagers will tell you, the monitoring and being there for your children is just as important when they are going through adolescence. You will have to determine the changing needs of your children now and over the next few years. If your children are juniors or seniors in high school or are attending college and not home very much, you may be able to be away from the home more, either traveling or working long hours outside the home. But if your children are younger, they may need you at home more, and you will need to assess those factors. Parents of school-aged children will attest to the demands on their time, just in driving children to and from activities and friends' houses. How much of your time your children need can best be determined by picking up signals from them in response to changes in your present and past availability. Your children will quickly let you know in some way if they feel like they are being ignored.

Lastly, you need to determine what needs of your family are currently being met or are not being met under your present situation. If you find that most all of your family's requirements are being met, a change may not be necessary. However, if you are picking up signals from your children or your husband that indicate there could be a problem in the making, then you must determine what needs are not being met. Usually the kinds of needs we are referring to here are not physical, since most parents usually try to ensure that their children's physical needs are met first. The kind of needs that usually get pushed aside are the emotional needs resulting from not enough time being spent with the parent.

This situation can result whether the mother works outside the home or not, even though one hears more about this lack of time when the mother does work outside the home. A friend of mine told me of a minister's wife who did not work outside the home, but felt as if she had to perform every favor asked of her, and that she had to be involved in every committee or group function. She soon found herself so busy meeting the church members' needs that she was neglecting her own family's needs. She had to learn to say "no" gracefully and give her family the same attention she gave outsiders. It was not until she started telling others "no" that she began to have the time she needed for her family.

Likewise, I know of women who do not work outside the home, but become involved in so many social activities that they do not spend any more time with their children than the woman who works outside the home. They may spend so much time on the phone planning activities or are out of the house involved in social organizations, that the kids actually do not receive any more attention. Because of this fact, we can not generalize one way or another by saying children's needs are being met or not being met just by the nature of the mother's work situation. The important consideration in this area is to determine whether your present situation is allowing you to do the things with your husband or children that you feel are necessary for their emotional stability and development, and whether you have time to get to know what each of your family member's needs are.

In connection with the idea of assessing your family's needs, you have to realize that the needs of each of your family members are different and are constantly changing. Thus, you have to constantly be analyzing these needs to see if they are being met. A career you have today may fit your family situation and needs, but tomorrow you could wake up and realize it no longer fits into the needs structure of your family. However, do not feel overwhelmed and think you will not find a career that can meet those needs, since there are some basic needs that you know are always going to be relevant. All children need love and support from their parents, which includes spending time with them. All children need to know that their parents will be there and are available for them in time of need. In addition, all children need their parents' involvement in the important aspects of their life, including school and extracurricular activities. If you find that your career or your social activities are not allowing you to meet these basic needs and others not specifically mentioned, then you probably should consider a change from your present situation.

In conclusion, it is important to remember that even though assessing yourself is a very crucial component, part of that analysis involves reviewing the current environment you have constructed for your life. As Mrs. Jumbo told Dumbo in the famous Walt Disney story,

"Don't let the hard times get you down. Just do your best, and someday you'll be flying high." I firmly believe that no one is totally stuck in her situation, and that she can bring about changes needed to meet her own and her family's requirements. However, before we move on to identifying your alternative courses of action, we need to review one more important aspect, which involves your current support network.

QUESTIONNAIRE FOR CHAPTER IV

ANALYZE YOUR SUPPORT NETWORK

Questions for all women:

Never Sometimes Frequently Always   1.   Do you live in close proximity to other family members or relatives?

Never Sometimes Frequently Always   2.   If you do not live near other family members, do you have close friends that are like family that you can ask for assistance?

Never Sometimes Frequently Always   3.   Are your relatives or close friends living nearby, physically able to assist in the care of your children?

Never Sometimes Frequently Always   4.   Do your relatives or close friends watch your children for you on a frequent basis?

Never Sometimes Frequently Always   5.   Do your relatives or close friends **offer** to take care of your children for you?

Never Sometimes Frequently Always   6.   Do your relatives or close friends assist you in taking your children to school or other activities?

Never Sometimes Frequently Always   7.   Do your relatives or close friends have schedules that allow them to assist with the caring for your children?

Never Sometimes Frequently Always   8.   Are you comfortable in calling upon your relatives and close friends for assistance?

Never Sometimes Frequently Always   9.   Do you feel guilty because you have strong family support for your children, but you still want to be the primary caretaker?

Never Sometimes Frequently Always   10.   Does your family make you feel you should be working outside the home more, because they are willing to take over some of the care for your children?

Never Sometimes Frequently Always   11.   Are you envious that other family members or close friends are more accessible to your children than you are?

Never Sometimes Frequently Always   12.   Would you be able to work outside the home at all, if it was not for the assistance from your relatives or close friends?

Questions for women who are married only:

| Never Sometimes Frequently Always | 13. | Is your spouse **willing** to assist with the care of your children? |

| Never Sometimes Frequently Always | 14. | Does your spouse assist with some of the responsibilities for the care of your children? |

| Never Sometimes Frequently Always | 15. | Does your spouse assist with taking your children to school or other activities? |

| Never Sometimes Frequently Always | 16. | Does your spouse have a job that takes him out-of-town, thus he cannot be relied upon on a consistent basis for support? |

| Never Sometimes Frequently Always | 17. | Do you wish that your spouse was more observant of the times in which you need some assistance? |

| Never Sometimes Frequently Always | 18. | Do you mind asking your spouse for help? |

| Never Sometimes Frequently Always | 19. | Would you be able to work outside the home at all, if it was not for the assistance from your spouse? |

CHAPTER IV

ANALYZE YOUR SUPPORT NETWORK

In the second chapter, we examined ourselves to try to determine what choices we wanted and could make in attempting to establish a personal balance between family and career. In the third chapter, we examined our present situation to determine what our existing family and work situation consisted of at present. In this chapter, we will look at another important aspect, the role our support network plays in determining the choices we will make. As one highly respected daycare provider told me, she felt the support network played a major role in determining which women seemed to be able to handle career and family successfully. In her opinion, those women who always seemed stressed were that way because in many cases, they did not have much assistance in taking care of the children. Because of the important role a support network plays in meeting family needs, we could not discuss making choices affecting our families without considering this aspect.

First, we need to define a support network. A support network in the family sense involves all those persons who are available or would be available to help assist with the responsibilities associated with raising children. In many cases for a woman, her husband is the first link in her support network. After her husband would usually come other family members such as grandparents, aunts or uncles, brothers or sisters, etc. Next in line would come close family friends, neighbors, baby-sitters, parents of school mates, etc. The support network for every women is different because many factors play into its development. A support network can help to alleviate some of the pressures on a woman by giving her options and possible time off from all the responsibilities of being sole provider for her children. The first thing every woman needs to determine is what and who is part of her support network.

In trying to determine and establish a support network, every woman will need to realize that there are true members of their support network and those who offer to be available but rarely ever are. This may be through no fault of their own, but due to circumstances which arise, such as working out-of-town, traveling, etc. Because not everyone will really be available or a woman will not always feel comfortable in calling on some members of her proposed network, she will need to take a hard and realistic look at her support network before she makes her choices regarding how much time she will need to be available herself.

After completing the analysis of the support network, a natural conclusion can be formed that if the network turns out to be small and not responsive, a woman will have to be more readily accessible, thus her choices of career could be limited. On the other hand, if there is a strong and responsive support network, then the woman would be more free to select careers that could involve travel or more time spent away from home. However, just because the support network is strong does not mean a woman has to or wants to work in a demanding career or be away from the home at all.

I have a strong support network, in that my husband rarely is out-of-town and is a big help if I should need it. He takes my two older sons to school every day on his way to work. In addition, my mother and father-in-law live close to the preschool and are retired so they are ready and have been very willing to help. I also have a brother and sister-in-law who both work, but in a bind would be willing to help. There are also a couple of close family friends that I can call on. I am also fortunate in that I have a good baby-sitter who lives down the street. In addition, even though my mother lives about three hours away, she has come to help me when I have needed her. But even though I am very fortunate to live near some of my family and have a good support network, it still does not change the fact that I want to be able to respond when my children need me and to call on those people only in a time of emergency. As a matter of fact, I just went through a time period prior to making the job change I have already discussed in this book, when I leaned on my support network very heavily. Between the travel and long hours, my husband, mother-in-law, baby-sitter and others, provided much love and support to my children when I was away. However, this situation was not satisfactory to me.

So even though you have a strong support network, you may still want to work in the home or only in a part-time situation. Your support network should not be, in any case, a driving force that causes you to feel as though you should be in a demanding career. The only reason the support network is mentioned in this book is that, without one you may have your choices limited.

If she determines that she will not have much assistance from her support network, the woman who chooses to have a family will have to realize that her career choices may be limited, and must factor this reality into her decisions concerning family and career. Unfortunately, those women who live away from their parents and other family members but still desire a career may be more limited in their options than a woman with family support nearby.

CHAPTER V

DETERMINE YOUR ALTERNATIVES

Once you have completed the analysis discussed in the first four chapters, you should feel you are on your way to taking hold of your life and designing it to your own specifications. The analysis of all the factors previously discussed is the hardest part of this task and now we can move forward to discuss what happens next. You obviously are going to have to make some hard choices and implement an action plan. However, before any woman can make her own choices, she needs to have recognized all her alternatives. While we will make some general statements here concerning alternatives, each woman must realize she will be faced with a unique set of alternatives based on the facts underlying her present situation and her own emotional psyche.

One of the first alternative choices a woman must make relates to whether she will pursue a job outside the home. If a woman is working outside the home, by now she should have determined why she is working. For many women there will be no alternative choice as to whether they will work outside or inside the home. As previously mentioned, it is a fact of life that in today's society, many women have to work for financial reasons. As we also discussed, some women have an emotional need that a career fills for them; thus, the option of working outside the home or inside the home may not really be an issue. However, we must all realize that this is one alternative choice that may be available in some situations and must be addressed first before we go any further.

If you do have as an alternative the option to work inside the home and you choose that option, then you must move to the second alternative you will be facing. **Is there a need to cut back certain items in your budget due to the loss of any income associated with**

working inside the home? Speaking from the experience of one who took a reduction in income to be able to do some of my work inside the home, this review is not a pleasant experience. As some people have said, it is always harder to cut back than to increase your spending, and I believe most people spend in relationship to their income level. I know there were a few areas we had to cut back in, but we also realized a reduction in spending due to having more time at home to cook meals and more time to shop for bargains instead of buying on impulse or at the last minute. In addition, you can save on the expense of hiring baby-sitters if you have more time at home and to finish your required errands. So even though you may have to cut back, you will be surprised at how much you will save just from not having to spend as much time away from home.

In addition, if you have determined that you have the alternative of staying home and that you are inclined to pursue that alternative, then you will need to review your elective engagements, social activities, and community involvement to determine if they are conflicting with the needs of your family. Here again, it will be hard to say no to some of the organizations you have worked so hard for, but most people will understand if they know you are trying to make the choices necessary to meet your family needs. Realize, too, that you may be on the receiving end of some hostile comments from women who are envious of your resolve to find more time for your family. Just keep in mind that these are your personal alternatives and you will be making choices based on a thorough self-analysis and review of your family's needs.

If you feel that working inside the home is not an alternative for you, whether as a telecommuting-type worker or as a stay-at-home mom, then you must look at a different set of alternative choices based on those available to a woman working outside the home. Most of the alternatives these women face relate to the career choices they must make, including hours, travel, distance from home, etc. One alternative relates to a full-time versus part-time status. Here again, this may not be an option for some women due to financial reasons. They may not only need the extra income from full-time employment, but also the benefits that are not available to many part-time employees such as health insurance, retirement, vacation, etc.

If a woman decides that part-time employment is an option for her, then she must weigh the advantages and disadvantages of part-time versus full-time and how this decision will affect her ability to meet her family's needs. Obviously, part-time employment allows more flexibility in hours and time at home. However, part-time employment sometimes does not pay as well, and may not offer the career advancement a woman may deem important. Another alternative along the lines of part-time employment could involve two part-time jobs instead of one full-time job, so that a decrease in finances does not result. However, a woman has to be organized to be able to keep the job duties separated and to keep track of hours worked at both job sites. By doing two part-time jobs, a women may be able to schedule work around children's' activities. For example, most of the time I work two part-time jobs. One job requires some work in the office, while allowing some work to be performed at home. The other job involves teaching college classes that can scheduled by semester to meet my personal itinerary. These two part-time jobs do not tie me down to an office for a set period of time such as to 5:00 p.m. My afternoons are free to pick up my children from school and I can attend field trips within certain constraints. Most managers feel differently about part-time workers and know that they will not always be available at their beckoned call. They learn to work within the part-time person's schedule, rather than expecting the part-time person to wait on them and be accessible at all times. Thus, when a child gets sick or is out-of-school for the day, they are not as resentful that the employee is not in the office. I find scheduling days off is easier too, as long as the deadlines of the job are met.

Another alternative relates to the type of job the woman chooses. Some jobs are more conducive to family situations than others just by the nature of the jobs themselves. Teaching school is one example of a job that fits well into a family situation. A day-care provider could be another example, along with some public and state office jobs that involve more time off for holidays and vacations. Other jobs can still be managed but will take more time and organization on the part of the parents to make them work. An airline stewardess is one job that becomes more difficult when you have children due to the distance factor and the working hours. Other jobs such as traveling sales also become more difficult when children are involved. Because you have already reviewed your present situation, you know whether your current career path fits into your ideal family setup. If you have found that a change in career is necessary, be careful in the selections you make by considering first the nature of the new job itself.

Job alternatives also involve factors such as commuting time, distance from the children's activities, out-of-town travel, hours, etc. Each of these alternatives should be considered in conjunction with your analysis. You may decide that a job which requires long hours or overtime will not fit into your family situation; so, you will narrow your scope on potential jobs. In addition, you may not want to spend an hour a day commuting, so you limit the geographic range of potential employers. Where your children attend school or will be participating in outside activities presents a consideration when evaluating alternative job sites, since you do not want to be constantly stressed at your job because you know how long it will take you to maneuver around once you have completed your work day. In some cases, these distance considerations could limit your involvement in school functions or your ability to do special activities with your children such as eating lunch with them at school. From personal experience with my son, I can tell you those thirty minute lunches that I periodically spend with him at school mean a lot to him, and other children are aware whose parents come to the school and whose do not.

In addition, a parent's attendance on field trips or at special events is also very important to a child's emotional development. One of the reasons behind my leaving my former job was that it did not allow me to meet my family responsibilities, including giving me time to attend field trips or to visit my son's school. In addition, the job involved out-of-town travel, which was sometimes hard on my husband and children. Being out-of-town also is hard on a mother when she has to miss her child's important events because she is called to work away from the home. I know that on one business trip, I had to miss the fall carnival at my son's school. Luckily, my husband was able to take him even though I truly desired to be there. In my former position, the out-of-town travel was such that I never knew exactly when I would be home. My children never knew who would show up to pick them up or when their mother would be home. Because of the uncertainty of my arrival, the evenings at home would already start out stressed. Especially when last minute trips out-of-town become necessary, the family unit becomes strained because no one has had time to make preparations for one member to be unavailable.

The one factor that may become stressful to many mothers who truly love to work, but put their family first, is that their alternatives become limited. This fact becomes even more important as the size of the family grows. One child can be shuffled around much easier than two or three. But you need to ask yourself, do you really want any of your children shuffled around? Since you should have already answered this question, you probably have realized that your family choices may have limited your career alternatives for awhile. I believe a woman can "Have it all," but maybe not all at one time. Maybe for the present, your career has to take a back seat to your family. The important thing to keep in mind is that you can resume your career at any time, whereas you can not reverse your children's growth and development and make up the activities and events you may miss. As the working world will always be in need of good workers, you do have a choice of which aspects of your life to which you want to devote your time and energy. Keep in mind that most of the situations we get stressed over are only temporary in nature.

CHAPTER VI

MAKE YOUR CHOICES

In the last chapter, we discussed how to determine your
alternatives so you can make informed choices.   In this chapter, we
will discuss making the choices among all the alternatives. One would
think this decision would be very straightforward, once you have
decided what you want. However, for many women, actually making
these choices and then implementing an action plan is almost as hard or
harder than the evaluations she has already performed. The truth of the
matter is that the evaluations are already inside each of us; we just have
to bring them to the surface. To make the choices means to actually
act upon the feelings inside of us, which may be met with resistance
from well-meaning people and could at some point be unpleasant. A
woman has to be firm as she makes these choices to ensure that they
are in fact her choices made with conviction. To take a quote from

Margaret Wise Brown's <u>Pussy Willow</u>, "Everything that anyone would ever look for is usually where they find it." We as women have to make it our resolve to find "it."

One of my first words of advice to any woman as she embarks upon this decision making process is to realize that once she has made her decision, she should never look back. A local minister preached on this issue one day by saying that if you always drove your car by looking into your rear view mirror, think of all the things you would miss seeing . My father has told me this same thing several times in my life when I have had to make some key decisions that would affect my future. This is not to say that you should not learn from the past, but that you should not let the past dictate your future. None of us will ever know if we made the right decision in every instance, so we should not keep second guessing a decision we have made. We should make the decision and move forward.

Remember, as you are making these decisions, what your desired balance between family and career is, and what alternatives are available to you within this scenario. Once I identified what I deemed to be my balance, I knew my first decision would involve leaving my current job. Once I moved past that decision, I had to decide what kind of job I could perform that would utilize my education and training, while at the same time give me the flexibility I would need. For me that involved forgetting the notion of full-time employment that would tend to make it mandatory for me to work in an 8-to-5 environment. I was fortunate in that my husband's job afforded us the benefits that allowed me to leave a full-time status behind. I ended up accepting a job part-time that allowed a flexible schedule, while doing some teaching and contract work to help supplement the decreased income.

While making your decision, it is helpful to make a family budget so that you are well aware of the financial needs of your employment situation. In addition, do not forget to factor in the employee benefits issue if that is a factor for you. The last thing any woman wants to do is to add more stress to her family in an effort to improve the quality of life. Losing income and benefits can be traumatic for a family if compensating support is not in place. As discussed earlier, some adjustments to your standard of living may be possible, but other adjustments will require buy-in from the other members of the family. Do not fail to factor in the financial concerns that may arise as a result of your decisions so that you may address them at the proper time. They should not dictate your decision-making process, but they should be thoroughly identified and addressed. Also consider the money that will be saved because of your proposed job change. Car expenses, such as gas and maintenance, may decrease because of less time spent commuting. By working my part-time jobs, I have saved the costs associated with after-school care, which can be substantial when you factor in three children. In addition, you may be able to reduce some costs associated with household help, because you can be home more to complete some of the tasks yourself. As I mentioned earlier, baby-sitting costs can decrease because you do not have to be away from home as much.

Lastly, remember to make your choices as soon as possible after you have completed the analysis phase of this process. The longer you wait to make decisions based on the evaluations performed earlier, the less likely you are to make the tough choices needed. All of us seem to be able to act when there is sufficient momentum, but find it much harder when the momentum has slowed. In my opinion, within a month after performing the evaluations discussed, a women should have outlined the key choices she will make. Most of these decisions will have already been identified, and possibly even noted, during the earlier phases. If so, consider yourself lucky because then you are ready to move into the implementation phase. If you have not previously recorded them, go ahead and do it now as soon as you finish reading this chapter. I recommend they be written down before you move on so that they do, in fact, get made. If you do not make the

tough choices, than you will not realize the full benefits of this book.

CHAPTER VII

FORM & IMPLEMENT AN ACTION PLAN

To coin a phrase we have all heard, "now is the time to put your money where your mouth is." You have performed the analysis and made your tough choices. Now you have to decide how you are going to carry out your decisions and make this new life you desire a reality. Many people are good theorists but cannot put their words into actions. We want action, so that we can achieve the desired results of a balanced lifestyle. The question arises, "How do you get started?"

First, you must be committed to force the change you need. At this time, you will be expressing verbally and in your actions the choices you have made. Others are probably not even aware of the fact that you have spent countless hours getting to this point. All of your self-analysis comes down to this point in your life. You can ignore it or you can act upon it, but the tenacity to act will have to come from within yourself. Do not expect others to naturally embrace your actions. Whether you are a passive person or aggressive person, you will most likely catch those close to you off guard. Keep the commitment strong within yourself to make these changes; because if others catch you wavering, they may not realize how much these choices mean to you. Your life is what you make it, and now is your time to make it happen.

Second, review the list of choices you made and what actions it will take to carry through with your decisions. Prioritize them by their significance to you and then attempt to place them in some sort of logical or chronological order of events. By doing so you may have already formulated an action plan. If you decide you want to chaperone more of your child's field trips, but your job does not provide you with flexibility to take needed time off, then that may mean requesting a change in your job situation. If this request is not acknowledged, then you obviously are going to have to consider a job

change, possibly leaving your present employer. This job change must

come, before you are able to attend the field trips. If some sort of

outside income from you is needed for your household, then you may

have to start immediately looking for another job. All of these events

will logically have to occur before you can count on being available for

one of those field trips.

Because each situation is different, there is not one blueprint for

how to carry out your decisions. It is unfortunate that there is not a set

of plans, because it would take a lot of the trial and error out of our

action plans and probably prevent some of our mistakes. You will find

that usually once you have listed your choices, a natural order of events

will be revealed. Look for an obvious flow and try not to make this

process too complicated. Before you can act, you have to have an

action plan that involves an orderly sequence of events. Every

touchdown in a football game could not have resulted if it was not for a set of plays that occurred in a certain order. For you to be successful,

you will also need a plan that includes a step-by-step approach. An

example of an approach is illustrated below:

1. Determine if a job change is needed and request it.

2. If the request is not acknowledged, search out other job
    opportunities.

3. Be specific with future employers about your job
    requirements.

4. Locate the job opportunity you desire and receive an offer
    of employment.

5. Accept new offer and quit other job.

6. Identify personal activities at which attendance is desired.

7. Schedule the activities.

Third, before you get started, explain to those people that mean

the most to you what you are trying to do. These people include your family members, close friends, and others whose support and advice you may need later. You may want to share this book or any notes that you have taken with them. Either way, you need to recap the self-analysis you have gone through and any significant realizations you have made about yourself, your family, your job, or your environment. I would advise providing them with a list of the alternatives you were able to come up with and the choices you made amongst the alternatives. You may also want to provide them with a copy of the step-by-step approach discussed above. Before you begin your conversation, make sure you have your audience's complete attention with no other distractions. Let them know that these are your choices and that you intend to stick with them. Make sure your body language agrees with the words you are speaking. Look them straight in the eyes, stand tall, and keep your head up and your shoulders high. At the end of the conversation, they must understand the reasons behind why you feel these changes are necessary and the realization that you will not rest until you have carried through with your decisions. It is up to you whether you have allowed or will allow these people to have input into the decision itself. However, if you allow their input, remember the bottom line is that the decision is yours to make and yours to live by. You may find it easier at this point to not even allow any input, if you fear your own judgment could become clouded. As Robert Louis Stevenson stated, "To become what we are capable of becoming is the only end of life." If you have accomplished these goals, then you need to pat yourself on the back for you have completed an important part of the implementation process.

Fourth, take your list of ordered choices and develop an outline that will be your own personalized blueprint for a successful lifestyle. Start working your list in order by addressing the first item. Make sure that item is resolved before moving to your next item. If your choice involves more time with your children, which subsequently means a job change, then you must find a new job first. Once you have found your new job and quit your old job, you can determine how best to spend the time with your children. Now you have options, but it took some action on your part that occurred in an orderly fashion. Go down your list item-by-item until you have addressed all of your choices. Try to remain as organized as possible as you go through this process, as it will help you ensure you do not overlook an important choice that must be addressed.

Fifth, develop a list of supporters that you can fall back on when the times get tough or the decisions you make are requiring some difficult actions on your part. This network of supporters can make the difference between successfully carrying out your plan and failure. Some supporters may immediately show their willingness to help, while other supporters may take some time before they truly lend their assistance. However, as every person needs a little encouragement along the way, you need to have some cheerleaders backing you even if they are late to join the game. Because you have already explained what you have decided to the significant people in your life, you have a natural place to start to find your supporters. Remember, though, not everyone will be supportive and you need to avoid discussing your endeavor with these naysayers while you are going through this process.

Sixth, keep your long range goal in mind, which is to obtain the balance between family and career that is necessary for your family's well-being. If we can keep the end product in the front of our minds at all times, then we will be less likely to get off track or down-hearted. I know as I have worked on this book over the past year, there have been times that I started to loose track of my one goal of completing this book. I had to stay determined to complete the book if it was ever to make it to press. During the end stages of the book, my brother laughed at me because I was working on changes to the book in the midst of five children playing. I would have to stop periodically to get juice, prepare food, break up a fight, etc. However, I was determined I would complete certain tasks with my book during that time so I worked on. If necessary, when you wake up each day, tell yourself, "I will get there. I will get my life in the order I need and have that balance."

Seventh, keep your attitude in check. I do not feel enough can be said about a person's attitude. My father has always said he would rather have a less-skilled worker with the right attitude, than the most-skilled worker with a poor attitude. As one famous saying goes, "Attitude is a little thing that makes a big difference." Often this quote is paired with a picture of a raindrop causing a swell in a pond. If you have the right attitude, you can accomplish great things. Most of us have seen examples of people who could have succeeded if they had only the right attitude. People have been turned down for promotions because management felt they had a poor attitude that would spread to others. Don't let your attitude keep you from accomplishing the changes you desire. You can do it, as long as you know you can. Think of the little train going up the hill that kept saying, "I think I can. I think I can. I know I can."

Lastly, be patient! Just as Rome was not built in a day, neither will your life become structured to your design at once. This process will most likely take some time and not happen overnight. Some choices you can implement immediately, while others will require you to carry through with some of your other choices first. I hope you will be so motivated from reading this book that you will want to get started right away and be anxious to see the results of all your hard work. However, I must caution you that anything worth having is worth taking the time necessary to make it happen. Do not become frustrated, but look to your supporters and give this process ample time to work. I think Samuel Johnson stated it best when he said, "Great works are performed not by strength but by perseverance."

CHAPTER VIII

SIT BACK AND ENJOY YOUR LIFE

Out of all the chapters in this book, this chapter is by far the easiest and most pleasurable to write. At this point in the process, the hard work is done. If you relate this process to an aerobic class, you have done the workout and are cooling down with a deep breath. Every woman who has gone through all the analysis, made the best choices she could from the alternatives she identified, and implemented her action plan, deserves the right to really take stock of her hard work and enjoy the results. The question is what kind of results can reasonably be expected?

As discussed before every thing about this process is individualized. Because of the unique nature of each woman's plan, the results will vary from very drastic to possibly minor. Most women will fall into the arena of significant changes in some areas with other areas possibly untouched. I can foresee, in the area of career possible job changes, more flexible working arrangements, shorter working hours, more work at home, etc. In the personal area, I can see more time spent with the family, more involvement with school activities, and more time for personal interests. You will determine the results that should be expected and if you stick to your goals, you will achieve them. Hallmark has put out a line of a cards geared towards the business environment called Hallmark Business Expressions. One of the cards discusses "Potential" and states:

Each day holds potential.

Potential for action or inaction

for passion or indifference

for hiding away our talents

or for using them to achieve

the greatest in ourselves.

Embrace each day.

Fulfill its potential.

So what do you do when the work is all done? First, realize that the work will never be completely done and thus keep working towards making your life complete each day so that you can realize its potential. Second, give yourself a strong pat on the back. If you can not appreciate yourself, others will not appreciate you either. Take some time off from your busy schedule to look back at the last few weeks or months of your life, depending on how long it took for your plan to come to fruition. Be sure to let the same people you confided in as you carried out your decisions know that you have completed most of your plan and that you appreciate their help. Just as it was important for you to obtain their advice earlier, you owe them the courtesy of knowing they have been an important part of this new life structure you have attained. I believe you can never tell people that you appreciate them enough, and actions speak louder than words. If you continue to keep these people as your allies, and if factors change later (and they will), then you will be more likely to obtain their support again. After all, besides yourself, a lot of these same people are the reasons why you are making the changes.

If you have ever heard the phrase "a rolling stone gathers no moss," you will know the next thing I am going to tell you. Once you have taken a little time to reflect on all the changes you have made, start moving with your new life. Start taking those kids to the zoo, or start going on those field trips with your children. Take that walk in the woods with your husband, or play that game with your children. Whatever you strove for, now is the time to enjoy it. You can look at yourself and say, "I have done well!" To quote the cat from one of the famous childhood books, The Cat in the Hat, "Look at me, look at me, look at me NOW! It is fun to have fun but you have to know how."